GUMBALLS & MONEY TREES

Story by Benjamin C. Dagley & Tracy Joy Jones
Illustrated by Jeanne Thompson

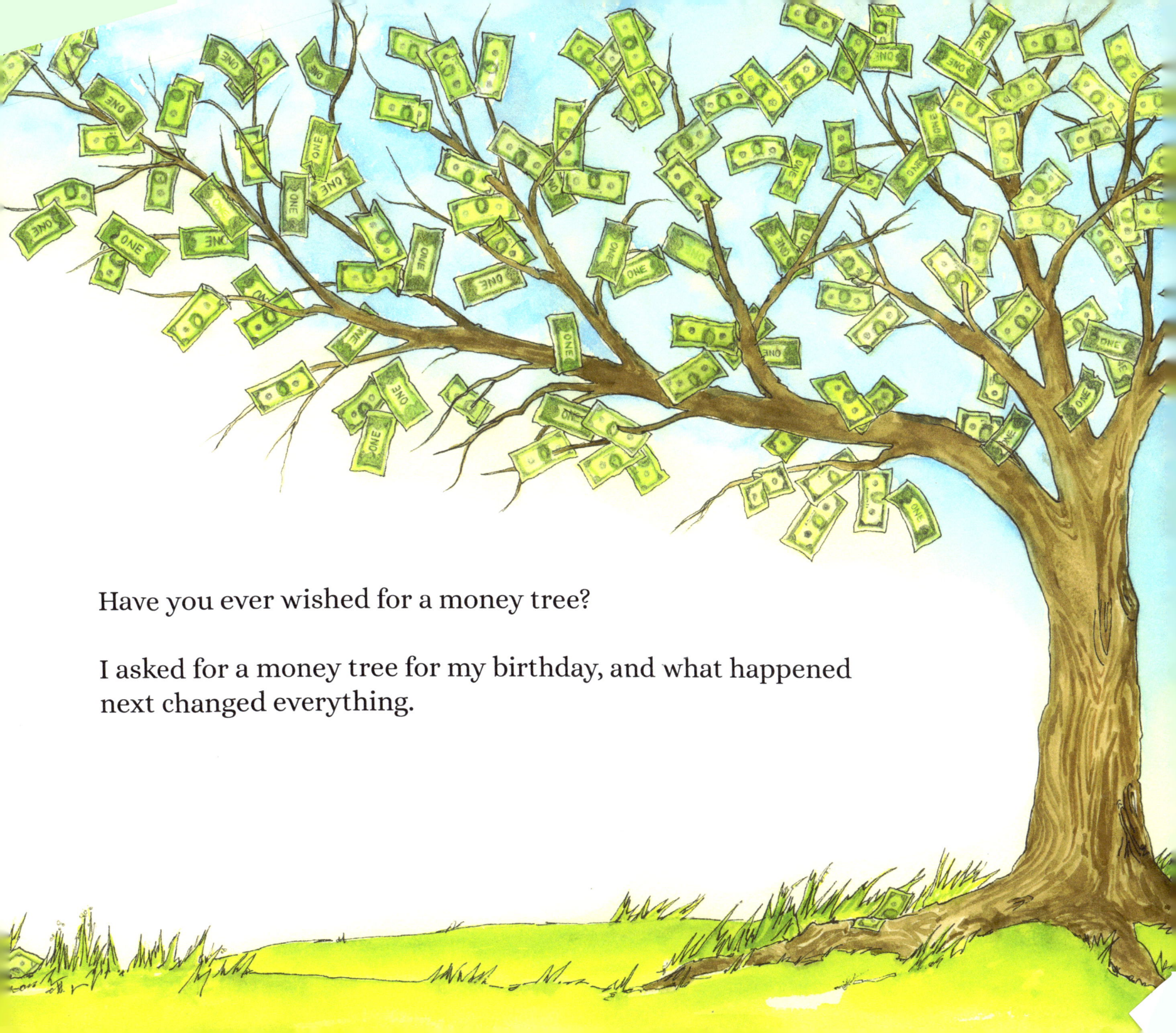

Have you ever wished for a money tree?

I asked for a money tree for my birthday, and what happened next changed everything.

It all started because I **LOVE** to shop!
But shopping takes money.

My family gave me money for my last birthday. But when it was gone, so was my shopping spree.

I needed a way to get more money.

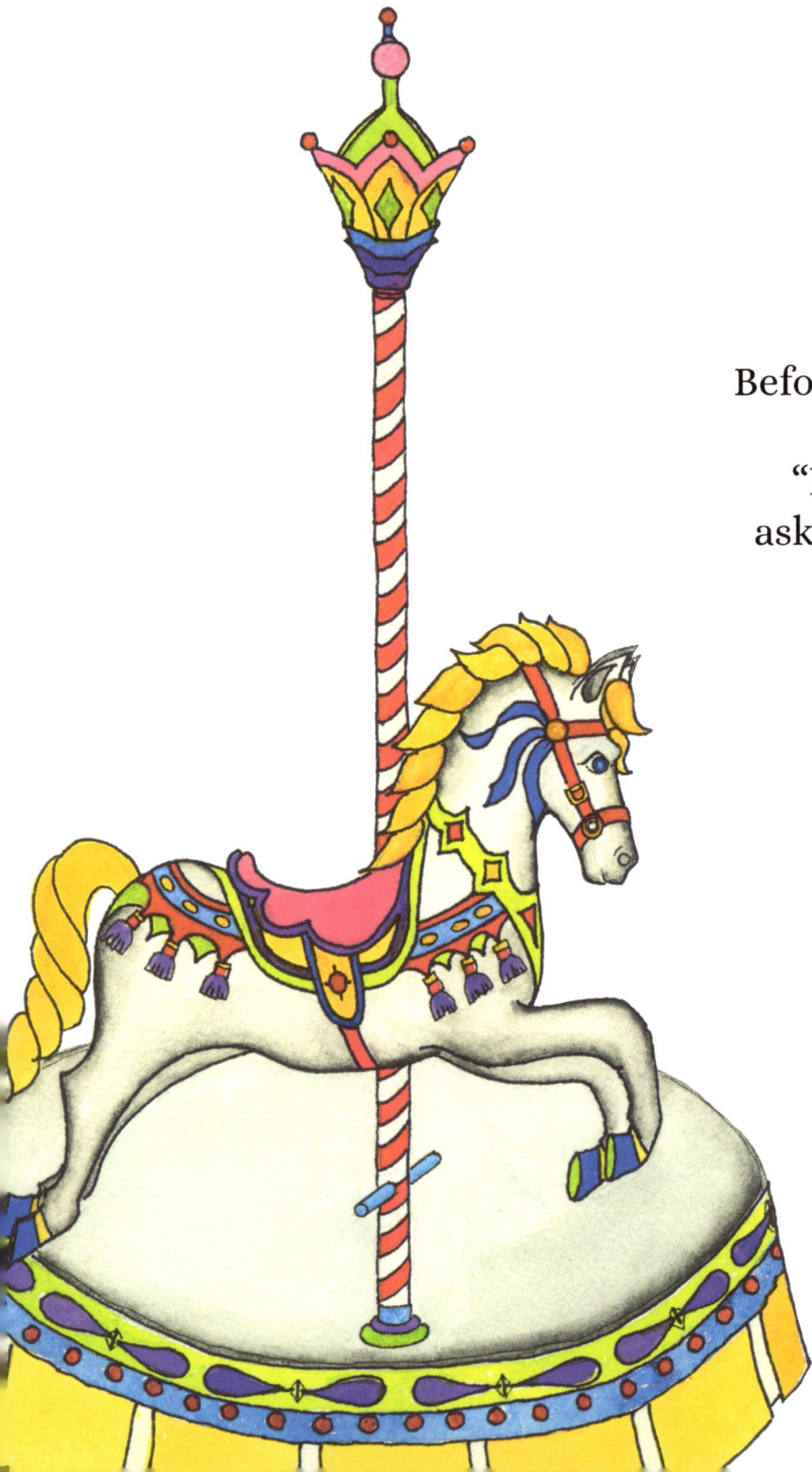

Before my next birthday, I had a *brilliant* idea.

"Mom? Dad?" I asked at dinner. "Instead of asking for a unicorn or a merry-go-round for my birthday, I've decided to ask for..."

Drum roll, please.

"...a MONEY TREE."

My dad smiled like he wanted to laugh.

"Why do you want a money tree, Tatum?" he asked.

"So I never have to ask for money for my birthday again. My money tree will make it for me."

He nodded, thinking for a moment. Then he leaned forward like he had something *really* important to tell me.

"Tatum, instead of a money tree, I'm going to give you something even better. I'm going to tell you the secret to making your money work for you."

"My money can work for me?" I asked.

My dad nodded. "The key is to spend your money on *assets*, instead of *liabilities*."

Assets? Liabilities? He lost me there.

"You see, Tatum, everything you own is either an asset or a liability. ASSETS put money into your pocket. LIABILITIES take money out of your pocket."

"Just like Heidi's little brother," I said, beginning to understand. "He is always taking money out of her purse without permission."

My best friend Heidi and I do NOT like *liabilities*.

My dad shook his head. "No, honey. That's not the kind of liability I'm talking about."

"Your toys and clothes are liabilities because buying them takes money out of your pocket. It's not a bad thing to have liabilities. You need clothes and food and books."

"And purses," I reminded him.

He smiled. "And purses. But the goal is to have your assets pay for your liabilities."

I thought about that for a moment. The only people who paid for anything around my house were my parents.

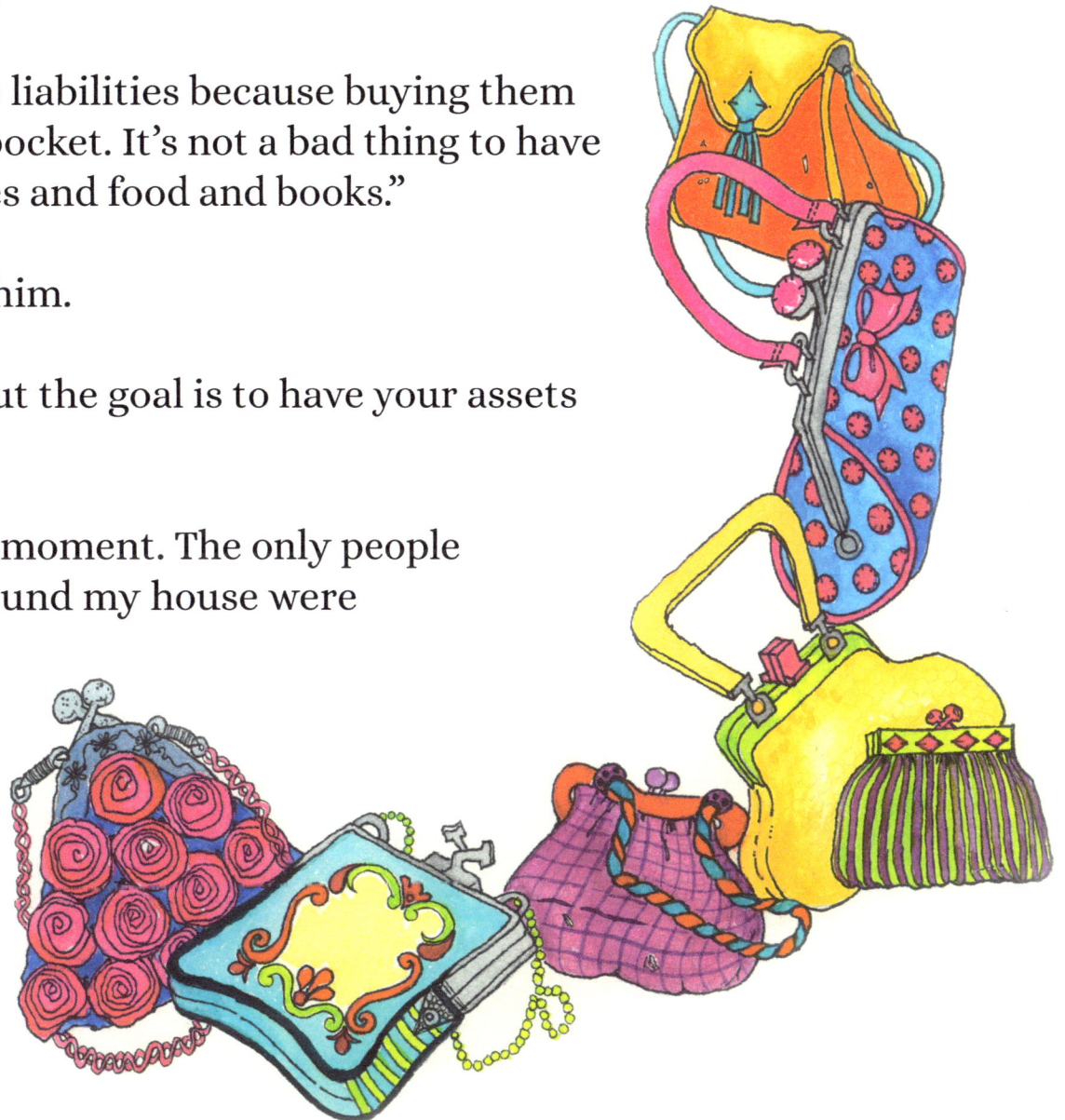

Yes! My parents were my assets. My cheeks pulled into a huge smile as I sat dreaming of my next shopping spree.

But my dad wasn't finished. "There are only three kinds of assets: businesses, stocks, and real estate."

"And parents?" I asked hopefully.

"No, Tatum. Your mom and I are not your assets."

POOF! There went my shopping spree plans. If my parents weren't my assets, I was back at the beginning without money or a money tree. I thought about my dad's words. I didn't know anything about stocks and real estate, but I knew businesses usually sold things.

I tried and tried to think of a business that would put money into my pocket instead of taking it out. By the time dinner was over, I gave up thinking. I needed help.

"Dad?" I said as he tucked me in that night. "I've decided what I want for my birthday."

"A money tree?" he guessed.

I shook my head.

"I want an asset."

Parents love it when you use their words. It makes them feel smart.

My dad smiled. "I think your mom and I can handle that. But are you sure that's what you want?"

"Definitely!" I answered with a smile.

The morning of my birthday, I couldn't
wait to see what my asset would be.

Maybe I would get a business that gave
me purses or books. Maybe I would get
free donuts for life.

The surprise inside the tall, lumpy
present was even better than I had hoped.

I ripped through the wrapping paper
to find...

My very own gumball machine! Hooray! Free gum for life!

My mouth watered as I stared into the glass bowl full of brightly-colored gumballs.

"Tatum," my dad said quickly, "these gumballs aren't for you to eat. They're for you to sell. This is your asset."

Oh, no! All those beautiful gumballs, and I didn't get to eat them?

"You see, Tatum, the gumballs in your machine are like seeds," my dad explained. "What if a farmer ate all of his watermelon seeds instead of planting them in the ground to grow more watermelons?"

I wrinkled my nose. Why would anyone eat watermelon seeds? Besides, that would mean, "No more watermelons!"

"Exactly. A wise farmer plants the seed and then waits until the harvest to eat the fruit. The same is true with your gumball machine. Plant your machine, let it make money for you, and then you can buy gumballs to eat with that money."

Sometimes my dad makes so much sense he takes away all my arguments.

I looked at my gumball machine, imagining the round, sugary balls as seeds and myself as a farmer. I knew I had to wait.

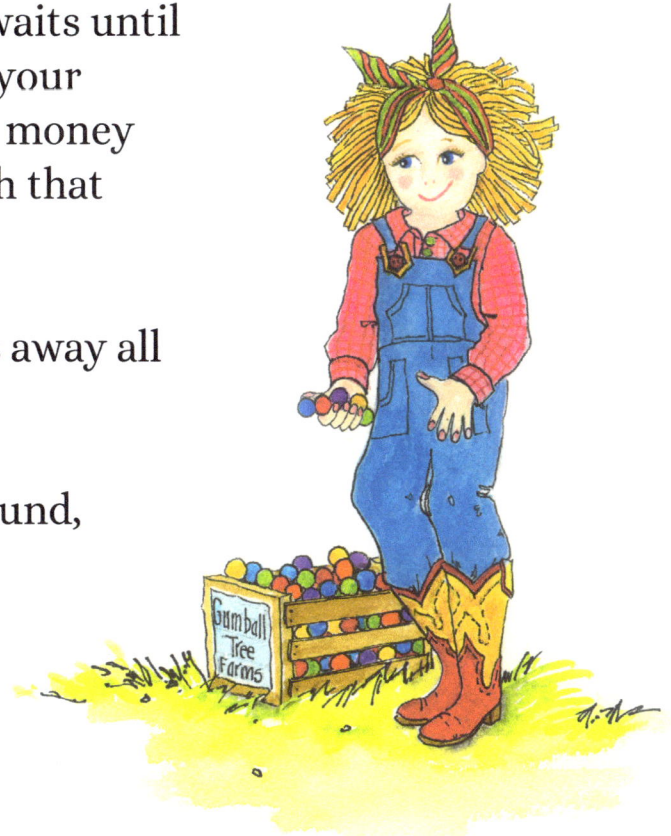

But where should I "plant" my gumball machine? I needed the perfect spot to grow nice, shiny quarters.

I found it at a coffee shop down the road from my house. The coffee shop owner agreed to let me put the gumball machine in his shop for free. I could hardly wait to see what would happen.

My dog, Chloe, and I walked to the coffee shop every day to see if anything was growing. Every day, there were fewer and fewer gumballs. I hoped that meant my money tree was growing and the quarters were piling up.

When the day finally came to check my gumball machine for quarters, I ran all the way there. Chloe didn't mind, but my dad had to hurry to keep up.

He helped me unlock the machine. When the door opened, I couldn't believe my eyes! I'd never seen so many quarters.

I put handful after handful into my sparkly purse.

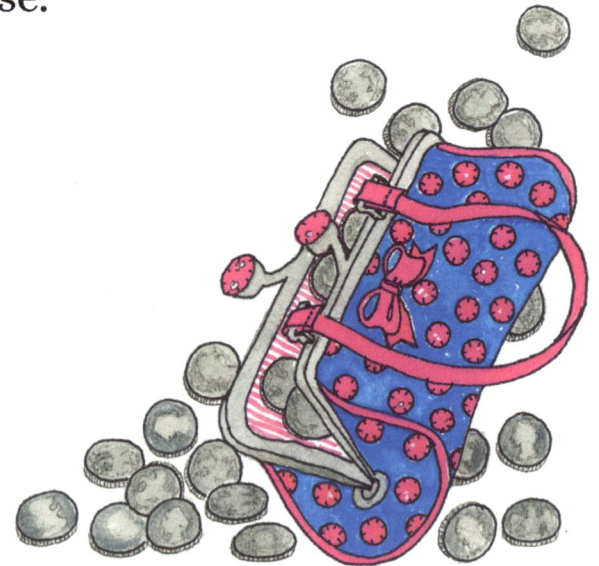

"Dad," I said as we walked home, my purse heavy with treasure, "I *really* like my asset."

My dad laughed, and Chloe barked in agreement.

When we got home, my parents helped me count the quarters. It added up to $95! That's more than I ever got for my birthday. I couldn't wait to go shopping.

"Okay, Tatum. Here's the real question," my dad said—just as I was planning all of the things I was going to buy. "Do you want to work for money, or do you want your money to work for you?"

I thought about it for a minute before answering, "I think I want my money to work for me."

My dad nodded. His smile said he was having another of those parenting moments.

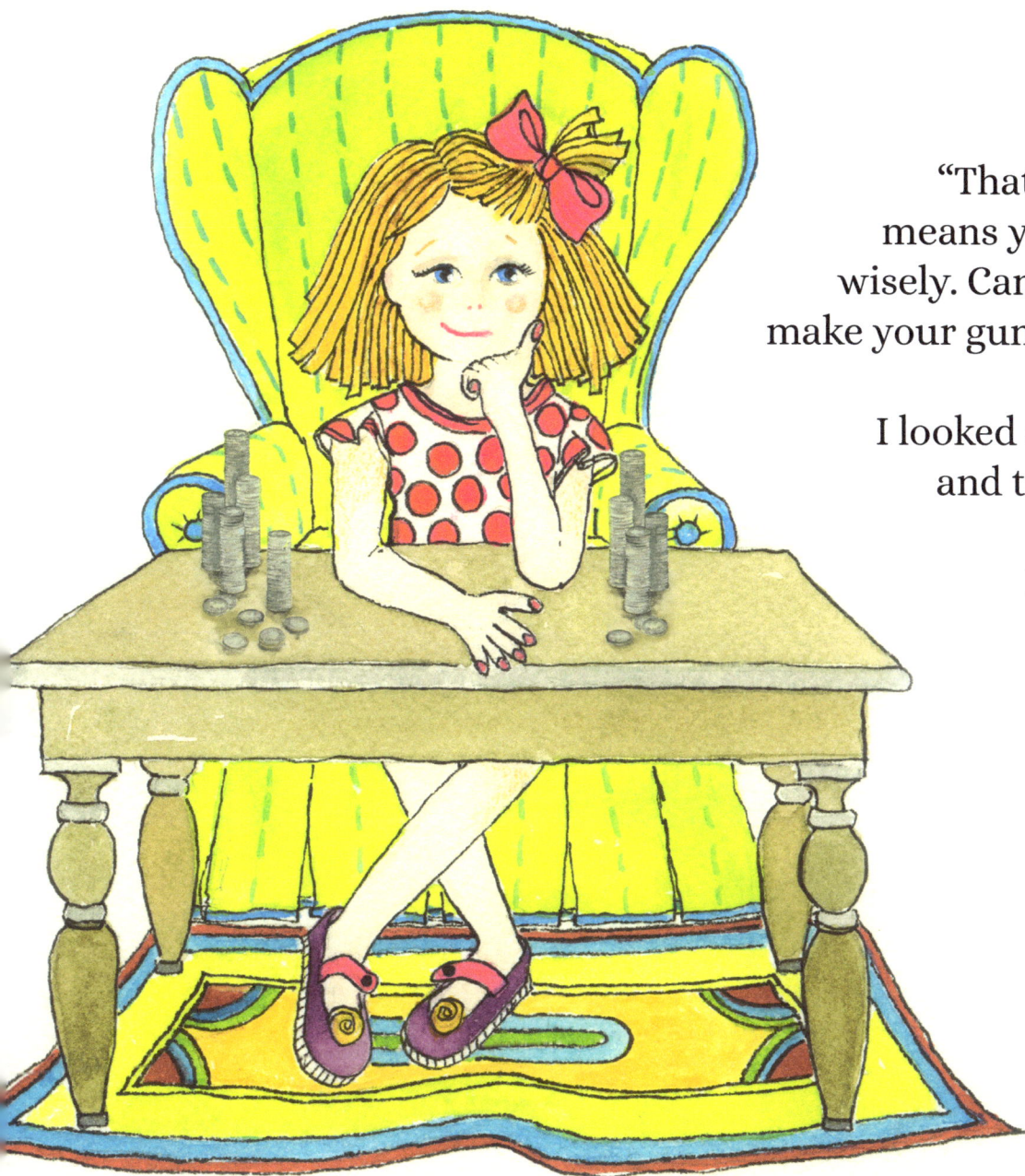

"That's good," he said, "because it means you want to use your money wisely. Can you think of a good way to make your gumball money work for you?"

I looked at the neat piles of quarters and tried to use my imagination.

How could piles of quarters lead to *more* piles of quarters?

25 cents

- 4 cents

──────────────

21 cents

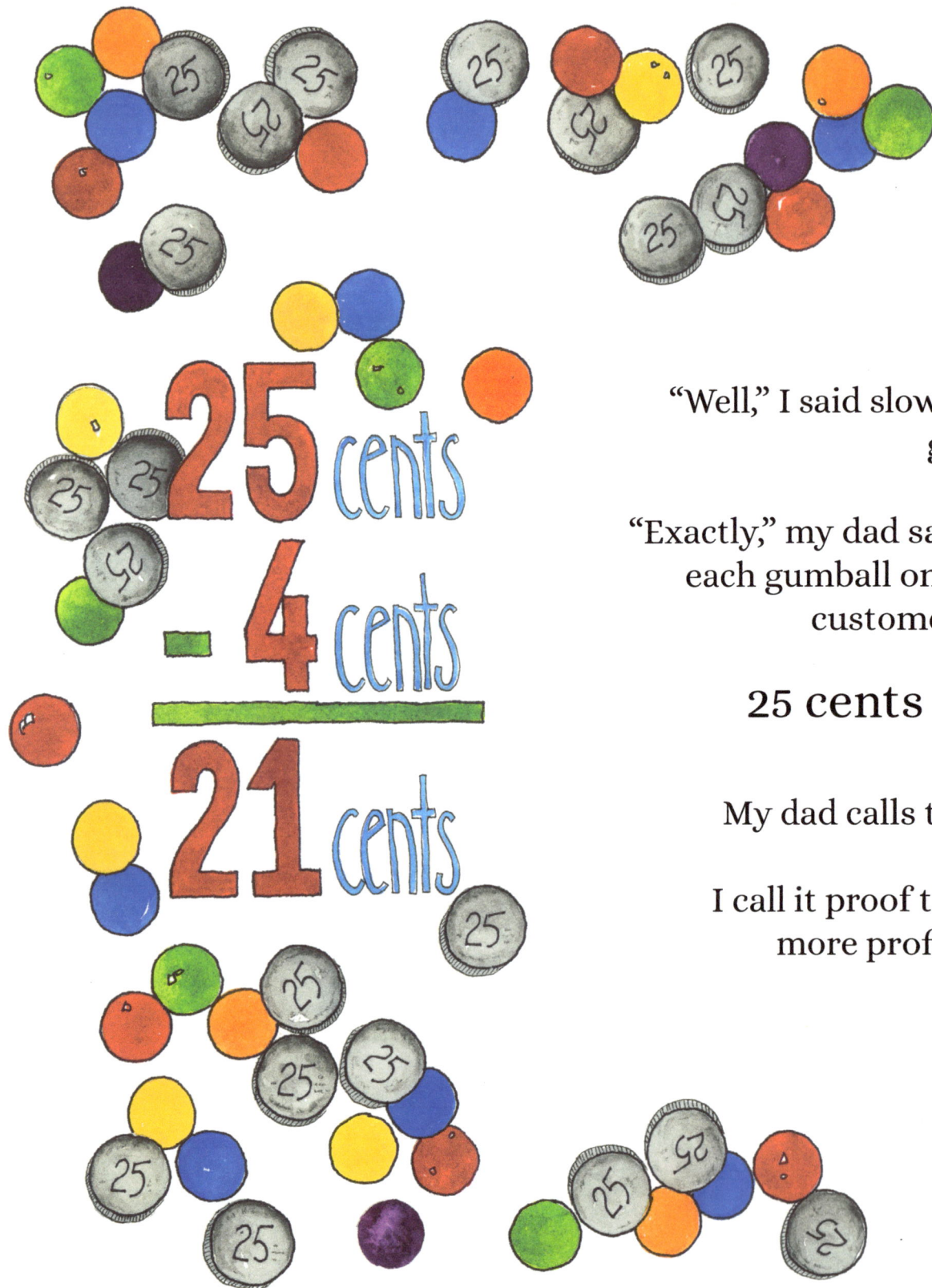

"Well," I said slowly. "Maybe I can buy more gumballs for my machine."

"Exactly," my dad said. He then explained that each gumball only cost me 4 cents, but my customers pay 25 cents a gumball.

25 cents - 4 cents = 21 cents

My dad calls the difference: PROFIT.

I call it proof that money trees exist. The more profit I make, the more money I have in my pocket.

If I buy more gumballs, I keep making profit.

Then I had another idea—an even *better* idea.

What if I bought more gumball machines with my profit?

And that's just what I did.

I now have *four* gumball machines, and they all make money for me —even when I'm not there!

I still get excited to collect so many shiny, silver quarters from my gumball machines.

Each time, I use some of the profit to buy more gumballs. I save some of the profit to buy a new machine. And I give some away because that's another lesson my dad taught me.

And with the rest, I get to buy *liabilities* like sparkly new collars for Chloe.

It turns out my mom and dad are
my greatest *assets* after all. Only instead of
money, they gave me something that makes
money for me. My dad calls me an *asset manager.*
I call myself a money tree farmer.

So, what are you waiting for?
Ask for an *asset* for your next birthday,
and become a business owner like me!

All you need is a goodie-filled
gumball machine.

Plant it in the right place,
water it with a little bit of patience,
and your own money tree will

grow and grow and grow.

As for me...

I'm going
SHOPPING!